Going to College on Uncle Sam's Dime

What Every Parent Needs to Know About the American Opportunity Tax Credits.

Robert A. Zappitelli, CFP, EA
John M. Zappitelli, CPA
Tax and Wealth Advisors

Going to College on Uncle Sam's Dime

Copyright © 2009 by (Robert A. Zappitelli and John M. Zappitelli)

ISBN (978-0-692-00658-0)

Printed in USA by 48HrBooks (www.48HrBooks.com)

This book is dedicated to our mom and dad,

Alfred and Antonietta Zappitelli.

Table of Contents

Acknowledgements

We'd like to acknowledge the government website that was the main source of our research for this book: Internal Revenue Service (www.irs.gov).

Visit our website at www.zappitellifinancial.com

Contact us at (440) 354-0375

or

zappitellifinance@sbcglobal.net

Preface

Zappitelli Financial Services was started in 1982 in the basement of the family-owned beverage store by John Zappitelli, a 1982 Kent State University accounting graduate.   His original accounts were small businesses in the immediate area, coupled with tax returns of family, friends and the accounting clients.   Brother Bob, a 1978 University of Akron graduate, joined John part-time in 1983 to help with the work load.

The beverage store moved to Concord, its present location, in 1983. Bob joined John on a fulltime basis in 1989.   They both became Enrolled Agents with the Internal Revenue Service in 1989. Bob earned his Certified Financial Planner (CFP) designation in 1996, and John became a Certified Public Accountant (CPA) in 1998.

Zappitelli Financial Services is a full service financial services company. We handle everything from new business start-ups, to payroll, bookkeeping and financial statements, to complete tax service, and even a mobile notary service.

Its newest branch offices are open and accepting new clients.   The Mentor-on-the-Lake office was opened in December 2008. This office is run by Josephine Zappitelli, a 2008 Notre Dame College graduate with a bachelor's degree in accounting. The Willoughby office was opened in August 2009 and is managed by Annie Zappitelli. Annie also graduated from Notre Dame College with an accounting degree.

Introduction

Since the American Recovery and Reinvestment Act of 2009 was enacted, our tax office has received numerous calls from taxpayers asking for clarification. Based on the interest, we decided to research the new tax credit and summarize our findings with this book. The first in our series of books is the Homeowner's Energy Credit. This book is the second in our series and will discuss the various education credits available, both new and old.

Chapter One: What's New

The American Recovery and Reinvestment Act of 2009 (ARRA) includes a provision for additional post-secondary tax credits for tax years 2009 and 2010. The ARRA expanded and renamed the already-existing Hope credit. More parents and students will qualify over the next two years for a tax credit, the American Opportunity Credit, to pay for college expenses.

The new credit modifies the existing Hope Credit for tax years 2009 and 2010, making the Hope Credit available to a broader range of taxpayers, including many with higher incomes and those who owe no tax. It also adds required course materials to the list of qualifying expenses and allows the credit to be claimed for four post-secondary education years instead of two. Many of those eligible will qualify for the maximum annual credit of $2,500 per student.

The full credit is available to individuals whose modified adjusted gross income is $80,000 or less, or $160,000 or less for married couples filing a joint return. The credit is phased out for taxpayers with incomes above these levels. These income limits are higher than under the existing Hope and Lifetime Learning Credits.

One change allows families saving for college to use popular 529 plans to pay for a student's computer-related technology needs. Under the other change, more parents and students will be able to use a federal education credit to pay part of the cost of college using the new American opportunity credit.

Chapter Two: American Opportunity/Hope Credit

For tax years 2009 and 2010, the following changes have been made to the Hope credit. The modified credit is also referred to as the American opportunity tax credit.

- The maximum amount of the Hope credit increases to $2,500 per student. The credit is phased out (gradually reduced) if your modified adjusted gross income (AGI) is between $80,000 and $90,000 ($160,000 and $180,000 if you file a joint return). *Exception*. For 2009, if you claim a Hope credit for a student who attended a school in a Midwestern disaster area, you can choose to figure the amount of the credit using the previous rules. However, you must use the previous rules in figuring the credit for all students for which you claim the credit.

- The Hope credit can now be claimed for the first four years of post-secondary education. Previously the credit could be claimed for only the first two years of post-secondary education.

- Generally, 40% of the Hope credit is now a refundable credit, which means that you can receive up to $1,000 even if you owe no taxes. However, none of the credit is refundable if the taxpayer claiming the credit is a child (a) who is under age 18 (or a student who is at least age 18 and under age 24 and whose earned income does not exceed one-half of his or her own support), (b) who has at least one living parent, and (c) who does not file a joint return.

- The term "qualified tuition and related expenses" has been expanded to include expenditures for "course materials." For this purpose, the term "course materials" means books, supplies, and equipment needed for a course of study whether or not the materials are purchased from the educational institution as a condition of enrollment or attendance.

Though most taxpayers who pay for post-secondary education will qualify for the American opportunity credit, some will not. The limitations include a married person filing a separate return, regardless of income, joint filers whose MAGI is $180,000 or more and, finally, single taxpayers, heads of household and some widows and widowers whose MAGI is $90,000 or more.

There are some post-secondary education expenses that do not qualify for the American opportunity credit. They include expenses paid for a student who, as of the beginning of the tax year, has already completed the first four years of college. That's because the credit is only allowed for the first four years of post-secondary education. Graduate students still qualify for the lifetime learning credit and the tuition and fees deduction.

Special rules apply to a student attending college in a Midwestern disaster area. For tax-year 2009, only, taxpayers can choose to claim either a special expanded Hope credit of up to $3,600 for the student or the regular American opportunity credit.

Chapter Three: Lifetime Learning Credit

For the tax year, you may be able to claim a lifetime learning credit of up to $2,000 ($4,000 for students in Midwestern disaster areas) for qualified education expenses paid for all students enrolled in eligible educational institutions. There is no limit on the number of years the lifetime learning credit can be claimed for each student and may be used for courses to acquire or improve job skills. The student does not need to be pursuing a degree or other recognized education credential. It is available for one or more courses.

A tax credit reduces the amount of income tax you may have to pay. Unlike a deduction, which reduces the amount of income subject to tax, a credit directly reduces the tax itself. The lifetime learning credit is a nonrefundable credit. This means that it can reduce your tax to zero, but if the credit is more than your tax the excess will not be refunded to you.

For 2009, the amount of your lifetime learning credit is phased out (gradually reduced) if your modified adjusted gross income (AGI) is between $50,000 and $60,000 ($100,000 and $120,000 if you file a joint return). You cannot claim a lifetime learning credit if your modified AGI is $60,000 or more ($120,000 or more if you file a joint return). The lifetime learning credit you are allowed may be limited by the amount of your income and the amount of your tax.

Generally, you can claim the lifetime learning credit if all three of the following requirements are met.

- You pay qualified education expenses of higher education. (Qualified education expenses paid by a dependent for whom you claim an exemption, or by a third party for that dependent, are considered paid by you.)
- You pay the education expenses for an eligible student.
- The eligible student is either yourself, your spouse, or a dependent for whom you claim an exemption on your tax return.

You cannot claim the lifetime learning credit for 2009 if any of the following apply.

- Your filing status is married filing separately.
- You are listed as a dependent in the *Exemptions* section on another person's tax return (such as your parents').
- Your modified adjusted gross income (MAGI) is $60,000 or more ($120,000 or more in the case of a joint return).
- You (or your spouse) were a nonresident alien for any part of 2009 and the nonresident alien did not elect to be treated as a resident alien for tax purposes.
- You claim the Hope Credit or a tuition and fees deduction for the same student in 2009.

For purposes of the lifetime learning credit, qualified education expenses are tuition and certain related expenses required for enrollment in a course at an eligible educational institution. The course must be either part of a postsecondary degree program or taken by the student to acquire or improve job skills.

Student-activity fees and expenses for course-related books, supplies, and equipment are included in qualified education expenses only if the fees and expenses must be paid to the institution as a condition of enrollment or attendance.

Qualified education expenses do not include amounts paid for insurance, medical expenses, student health fees, room and board, transportation or similar personal, living, or family expenses. This is true even in the amount must be paid to the institution as a condition of enrollment or attendance.

Chapter Four: Scholarships & Fellowships

A scholarship is generally an amount paid or allowed to, or for the benefit of, a student at an educational institution to aid in the pursuit of studies. The student may be either an undergraduate or a graduate. A fellowship is generally an amount paid for the benefit of an individual to aid in the pursuit of study or research. Generally, whether the amount is tax free or taxable depends on the expense paid with the amount and whether you are a degree candidate.

A scholarship or fellowship is tax free only if you meet the following conditions:

- You are a candidate for a degree at an eligible educational institution.
- You use the scholarship or fellowship to pay qualified education expenses.

An eligible educational institution is one that maintains a regular faculty and curriculum and normally has a regularly enrolled body of students in attendance at the place where it carries on its educational activities.

For purposes of tax-free scholarships and fellowships, qualified education expenses are for:

- Tuition and fees required to enroll at or attend an eligible educational institution.
- Course-related expenses, such as fees, books, supplies, and equipment that are required for the courses at the eligible educational institution. These items must be required of all students in your course of instruction.

19

However, in order for these to be qualified education expenses, the terms of the scholarship or fellowship cannot require that it be used for other purposes, such as room and board, or specify that it cannot be used for tuition or course-related expenses.

Qualified education expenses do not include the cost of room and board, travel, research, clerical help, and equipment and other expenses that are not required for enrollment in or attendance at an eligible educational institution. This is true even if the fee must be paid to the institution as a condition of enrollment or attendance. Scholarship or fellowship amounts used to pay these costs are taxable.

Chapter Five: Student Loan Interest

Generally, personal interest you pay, other than certain mortgage interest, is not deductible on your tax return. However, if your modified adjusted gross income (MAGI) is less than $75,000 ($150,000 if filing a joint return), there is a special deduction allowed for paying interest on a student loan (also known as an education loan) used for higher education. Student loan interest is interest you paid during the year on a qualified student loan. It includes both required and voluntary interest payments.

For most taxpayers, MAGI is the adjusted gross income as figured on their federal income tax return before subtracting any deduction for student loan interest. This deduction can reduce the amount of your income subject to tax by up to $2,500 in 2009. Your student loan interest deduction for 2009 is generally the smaller of $2,500 or the interest you paid in 2009. However, this amount may be gradually reduced or eliminated based on your filing status and modified adjusted gross income.

The student loan interest deduction is taken as an adjustment to income. This means you can claim this deduction even if you do not itemize deductions on Schedule A (Form 1040).

A qualified student loan is one you took out solely to pay qualified education expenses (defined later) that were:

- For you, your spouse, or a person who was your dependent when you took out the loan.
- Paid or incurred within a reasonable period of time before or after you took out the loan.
- For education provided during an academic period for an eligible student That was enrolled at least half-time in a degree program.

Loans from a related person or a qualified employer plan are not qualified student loans.

For purposes of the student loan interest deduction, qualified education expenses are the total costs of attending an eligible educational institution, including graduate school. They include amounts paid for tuition and fees, room and board, books, supplies and equipment, and other necessary expenses (such as transportation).

Chapter Six: Student Loan Cancellations

If you fulfill certain requirements, two types of student loan assistance may be tax free. They are student loan cancellation and student loan repayment assistance. Generally, if you are responsible for making loan payments, and the loan is canceled (forgiven), you must include the amount that was forgiven in your gross income for tax purposes. However, if your student loan is canceled, you may not have to include any amount in income. This section describes the requirements for tax-free treatment of canceled student loans.

To qualify for tax-free treatment, your loan must contain a provision that all or part of the debt will be canceled if you work for a certain period of time, in certain professions, and for any of a broad class of employers. The loan must have been made by a qualified lender to assist the borrower in attending an eligible educational institution.

Qualified lenders include the following:

- The government—federal, state, or local, or an instrumentality, agency, or subdivision thereof.
- A tax-exempt public benefit corporation that has assumed control of a state, county, or municipal hospital and whose employees are considered public employees under state law.
- An eligible educational institution, if the loan is made:
    - As part of an agreement with an entity described in (1) or (2) under which the funds to make the loan were provided to the educational institution, or
    - Under a program of the educational institution that is designed to encourage its students to serve in occupations with unmet needs or in areas with unmet needs where the services required of the students are for or under the direction of a governmental unit or a tax-exempt section 501(c)(3) organization. In satisfying the

service requirement, the student must not provide services for the lender organization.

Loan repayment assistance programs (LRAP) provide help in repaying student loans for those who work in public service occupations or in areas with unmet needs. Examples of such occupations are health care professionals in underserved areas, attorneys in legal-aid offices and prosecutor's or public defender's offices, and classroom teachers in subject areas with shortages.

An LRAP loan refinances your original student loan(s). After you work for a certain minimum period of time in a qualifying position, all or part of your student loan indebtedness is forgiven.

The amount of your loan that is forgiven is tax-free if the LRAP meets certain criteria. Repayment assistance received under the following programs has been determined to be tax free.

- National Health Service Corps (NHSC) Loan Repayment Program.
- State programs eligible for funds under the Public Health Service Act.
- Law school LRAP.

If your repayment assistance is from a source other than those listed, contact the program administrator to see if the LRAP qualifies for tax-free assistance. You cannot deduct the interest you paid on a student loan to the extent payments were made through your participation in the above programs.

Chapter Seven: Tuition and Fees Deduction

You may be able to deduct qualified education expenses paid during the year for yourself, your spouse or your dependent. You cannot claim this deduction if your filing status is married filing separately or if another person can claim an exemption for you as a dependent on his or her tax return. The qualified expenses must be for higher education.

The tuition and fees deduction can reduce the amount of your income subject to tax by up to $4,000. This deduction, reported on Form 8917, Tuition and Fees Deduction, is taken as an adjustment to income. This means you can claim this deduction even if you do not itemize deductions on Schedule A (Form 1040). This deduction may be beneficial to you if, for example, you cannot take the lifetime learning credit because your income is too high.

You may be able to take one of the education credits for your education expenses instead of a tuition and fees deduction. You can choose the one that will give you the lower tax.

Generally, you can claim the tuition and fees deduction if all three of the following requirements are met:

- You pay qualified education expenses of higher education.
- You pay the education expenses for an eligible student.
- The eligible student is yourself, your spouse, or your dependent for whom you claim an exemption on your tax return.

You cannot claim the tuition and fees deduction if any of the following apply:

- Your filing status is married filing separately.
- Another person can claim an exemption for you as a dependent on his or her tax return. You cannot take the deduction even if the other person does not actually claim that exemption.

- Your modified adjusted gross income (MAGI) is more than $80,000 ($160,000 if filing a joint return).
- You were a nonresident alien for any part of the year and did not elect to be treated as a resident alien for tax purposes.
- You or anyone else claims an education credit for expenses of the student for whom the qualified education expenses were paid.

Student-activity fees and expenses for course-related books, supplies and equipment are included in qualified education expenses only if the fees and expenses must be paid to the institution as a condition of enrollment or attendance. Personal, living, or family expenses, such as room and board, are not included.

The tuition and fees deduction is based on qualified education expenses you pay for yourself, your spouse, or your dependent for whom you claim an exemption on your tax return. Generally, the deduction is allowed for qualified education expenses paid in 2009 in connection with enrollment at an institution of higher education during 2009 or for an academic period beginning in 2009 or in the first 3 months of 2010.

You can claim a tuition and fees deduction for qualified education expenses paid with the proceeds of a loan. You use the expenses to figure the deduction for the year in which the expenses are paid, not the year in which the loan is repaid. Treat loan payments sent directly to the educational institution as paid on the date the institution credits the student's account. If your dependent pays qualified education expenses and you can claim an exemption for your dependent on your tax return, no one can take a tuition and fees deduction for those expenses. Neither you nor your dependent can deduct the expenses. For purposes of the tuition and fees deduction, you are not treated as paying any expenses actually paid by a dependent for whom you or anyone other than the dependent can claim an exemption. This rule applies even if you do not claim an exemption for your dependent on your tax return.

However, if your dependent pays qualified education expenses and no one can claim an exemption for your dependent on his or her tax return, your dependent can take a tuition and fees deduction for those expenses, even if they are paid with the proceeds of a student loan.

Chapter Eight: Coverdell Accounts

Coverdell savings accounts were created as an incentive to help parents and students save for education expenses. Unlike a 529 plan, a Coverdell ESA can be used to pay a student's eligible k-12 expenses, as well as post-secondary expenses. On the other hand, income limits apply to contributors, and the total contributions for the beneficiary of this account cannot be more than $2,000 in any year, no matter how many accounts have been established. A beneficiary is someone who is under age 18 or is a special needs beneficiary when the account is established.

Contributions to a Coverdell ESA are not deductible, but amounts deposited in the account grow tax free until distributed. The beneficiary will not owe tax on the distributions if they are less than a beneficiary's qualified education expenses at an eligible institution. This benefit applies to qualified higher education expenses as well as to qualified elementary and secondary education expenses.

Here are some things to remember about distributions from Coverdell accounts:

- Distributions are tax-free as long as they are used for qualified education expenses, such as tuition and fees, required books, supplies and equipment and qualified expenses for room and board.
- There is no tax on distributions if they are for enrollment or attendance at an eligible educational institution. This includes any public, private or religious school that provides elementary or secondary education as determined under state law. Virtually all accredited public, nonprofit and proprietary (privately owned profit-making) post-secondary institutions are eligible.
- Education tax credits can be claimed in the same year the beneficiary takes a tax-free distribution from a Coverdell ESA, as long as the same expenses are not used for both benefits.

- If the distribution exceeds qualified education expenses, a portion will be taxable to the beneficiary and will usually be subject to an additional 10% tax. Exceptions to the additional 10% tax include the death or disability of the beneficiary or if the beneficiary receives a qualified scholarship.

A Coverdell ESA is a trust or custodial account created or organized in the United States only for the purpose of paying the qualified education expenses of the designated beneficiary of the account. It can be opened at any bank or other IRS-approved entity that offers Coverdell ESAs. If your modified adjusted gross income (MAGI) is less than $110,000 ($220,000 if filing a joint return), you may be able to establish a Coverdell ESA to finance the qualified education expenses of a designated beneficiary. For most taxpayers, MAGI is the adjusted gross income as figured on their federal income tax return.

There is no limit on the number of separate Coverdell ESAs that can be established for a designated beneficiary. However, total contributions for the beneficiary in any year cannot be more than $2,000, no matter how many accounts have been established.

The document creating and governing the account must be in writing and must satisfy the following requirements.

1. The trustee or custodian must be a bank or an entity approved by the IRS.
2. The document must provide that the trustee or custodian can only accept a contribution that meets all of the following conditions.
   a. The contribution is in cash.
   b. The contribution is made before the beneficiary reaches age 18, unless the beneficiary is a special needs beneficiary.
   c. The contribution would not result in total contributions for the year (not including rollover contributions) being more than $2,000.

3. Money in the account cannot be invested in life insurance contracts.
4. Money in the account cannot be combined with other property except in a common trust fund or common investment fund.
5. The balance in the account generally must be distributed within 30 days after the earlier of the following events.

    a. The beneficiary reaches age 30, unless the beneficiary is a special needs beneficiary.

    b. The beneficiary's death.

For purposes of Coverdell ESAs, an eligible educational institution can be either an eligible postsecondary school or an eligible elementary or secondary school.

Eligible postsecondary school.   This is any college, university, vocational school, or other postsecondary educational institution eligible to participate in a student aid program administered by the U.S. Department of Education. It includes virtually all accredited public, nonprofit, and proprietary (privately owned profit-making) postsecondary institutions. The educational institution should be able to tell you if it is an eligible educational institution.

Certain educational institutions located outside the United States also participate in the U.S. Department of Education's Federal Student Aid (FSA) programs.

Eligible elementary or secondary school.   This is any public, private, or religious school that provides elementary or secondary education (kindergarten through grade 12), as determined under state law.

Table 7-2.Coverdell ESA Contributions at a Glance

Question	Answer
Are contributions	No.

31

deductible?	
Why should someone contribute to a Coverdell ESA?	Earnings on the account grow tax free until distributed.
What is the annual contribution limit per designated beneficiary?	$2,000 for each designated beneficiary.
What if more than one Coverdell ESA has been opened for the same designated beneficiary?	The annual contribution limit is $2,000 for each beneficiary, no matter how many Coverdell ESAs are set up for that beneficiary.
What if more than one individual makes contributions for the same designated beneficiary?	The annual contribution limit is $2,000 per beneficiary, no matter how many individuals contribute.
Can contributions other than cash be made to a Coverdell ESA?	No.
When must contributions stop?	No contributions can be made to a beneficiary's Coverdell ESA after he or she reaches age 18, unless the beneficiary is a special needs beneficiary.

The designated beneficiary of a Coverdell ESA can take a distribution at any time. Whether the distributions are tax free depends, in part, on whether the distributions are equal to or less than the amount of adjusted qualified education expenses (defined next) that the beneficiary has in the same tax year.

Table 7-3.Coverdell ESA Distributions at a Glance

Question	Answer
Is a distribution from a Coverdell ESA to pay for a designated beneficiary's qualified education expenses tax free?	Generally, yes, to the extent the amount of the distribution is not more than the designated beneficiary's adjusted qualified education expenses.
After the designated beneficiary completes his or her education at an eligible educational institution, can amounts remaining in the Coverdell ESA be distributed?	Yes. Amounts must be distributed when the designated beneficiary reaches age 30, unless he or she is a special needs beneficiary. Also, certain transfers to members of the beneficiary's family are permitted.
Does the designated beneficiary need to be enrolled for a minimum number of courses to take a tax-free distribution?	No.

Chapter Nine: Early IRA Distributions

Generally, if you take a distribution from your IRA before you reach age 59½, you must pay a 10% additional tax on the early distribution. This applies to any IRA you own, whether it is a traditional IRA (including a SEP-IRA), a Roth IRA, or a SIMPLE IRA. The additional tax on an early distribution from a SIMPLE IRA may be as high as 25%.

However, you can take distributions from your IRAs for qualified higher education expenses without having to pay the 10% additional tax. You may owe income tax on at least part of the amount distributed, but you may not have to pay the 10% additional tax. The part not subject to the additional tax is generally the amount of the distribution that is not more than the adjusted qualified education expenses for the year.

You can take a distribution from your IRA before you reach age 59½ and not have to pay the 10% additional tax if, for the year of the distribution, you pay qualified education expenses for:

- yourself,
- your spouse, or
- your or your spouse's child, foster child, adopted child, or descendant of any of them.

For purposes of the 10% additional tax, these expenses are tuition, fees, books, supplies, and equipment required for enrollment or attendance at an eligible educational institution. The expense for room and board qualifies only to the extent that it is not more than the greater of the following two amounts.

1. The allowance for room and board, as determined by the eligible educational institution, that was included in the cost of attendance (for federal financial aid purposes) for a particular academic period and living arrangement of the student.

2. The actual amount charged if the student is residing in housing owned or operated by the eligible educational institution.

To determine the amount of your distribution that is not subject to the 10% additional tax, first figure your adjusted qualified education expenses. You do this by reducing your total qualified education expenses by any tax-free educational assistance, which includes:

- Expenses used to figure the tax-free portion of distributions from a Coverdell education savings account (ESA),
- The tax-free part of scholarships and fellowships,
- Pell grants,
- Veterans' educational assistance,
- Employer-provided educational assistance, and
- Any other nontaxable (tax-free) payments (other than gifts or inheritances) received as educational assistance.

Do not reduce the qualified education expenses by amounts paid with funds the student receives as:

- Payment for services, such as wages,
- A loan,
- A gift,
- An inheritance given to either the student or the individual making the withdrawal, or
- A withdrawal from personal savings (including savings from a qualified tuition program (QTP)).

If your IRA distribution is equal to or less than your adjusted qualified education expenses, you are not subject to the 10% additional tax. If you received an early distribution from your IRA, you must report the taxable earnings on Form 1040. Then, if you qualify for an exception for qualified higher education expenses, you must file Form 5329 to show how much, if any, of your early distribution is subject to the 10% additional tax.

Chapter Ten: Savings Bonds

Generally, you must pay tax on the interest earned on U.S. savings bonds. If you do not include the interest in income in the years it is earned, you must include it in your income in the year in which you cash in the bonds.

However, when you cash in certain savings bonds under an education savings bond program, you may be able to exclude the interest from income. You may be able to cash in qualified U.S. savings bonds without having to include in your income some or all of the interest earned on the bonds if you meet the following conditions.

- You pay qualified education expenses for yourself, your spouse, or a dependent for whom you claim an exemption on your return.
- Your modified adjusted gross income (MAGI) is less than $84,950 ($134,900 if married filing jointly or qualifying widow(er)).
- Your filing status is not married filing separately.

A qualified U.S. savings bond is a series EE bond issued after 1989 or a series I bond. The bond must be issued either in your name (as the sole owner) or in the name of both you and your spouse (as co-owners).

The owner must be at least 24 years old before the bond's issue date. The issue date is printed on the front of the savings bond. The issue date is not necessarily the date of purchase—it will be the first day of the month in which the bond is purchased (or posted, if bought electronically).

Qualified education expenses include the following items you pay for either yourself, your spouse, or a dependent for whom you claim an exemption:

1. Tuition and fees required to enroll at or attend an eligible educational institution. Qualified education expenses do not include expenses for room and board or for courses involving

sports, games, or hobbies that are not part of a degree or certificate granting program.

2. Contributions to a qualified tuition program (QTP)

3. Contributions to a Coverdell education savings account (

You must reduce your qualified education expenses by all of the following tax-free benefits.

1. Tax-free part of scholarships and fellowships.

2. Expenses used to figure the tax-free portion of distributions from a Coverdell ESA.

3. Expenses used to figure the tax-free portion of distributions from a QTP.

4. Any tax-free payments (other than gifts or inheritances) received as educational assistance, such as:

   a. Veterans' educational assistance benefits,

   b. Qualified tuition reductions, or

   c. Employer-provided educational assistance.

5. Any expenses used in figuring the Hope and lifetime learning credits

You claim an exemption for a person if you list his or her name and other required information on Form 1040 (or Form 1040A), line 6c. If the total you receive when you cash in the bonds is not more than the adjusted qualified education expenses for the year, all of the interest on the bonds may be tax free. However, if the total you receive when you cash in the bonds is more than the adjusted expenses, only part of the interest may be tax free. The amount of your interest exclusion is gradually reduced (phased out) if your modified adjusted gross income is between $69,950 and $84,950 (between $104,900 and $134,900 if your filing status is married filing jointly or qualifying widow(er)).

You cannot exclude any of the interest if your modified adjusted gross income is equal to or more than the upper limit. The phaseout, if any, is figured for you when you fill out Form 8815.

Use Form 8815 to figure your education savings bond interest exclusion. Enter your exclusion on line 3 of Schedule B (Form 1040), Interest and Ordinary Dividends, or Schedule 1 (Form 1040A), Interest and Ordinary Dividends for Form 1040A Filers. Attach Form 8815 to your tax return.

Chapter Eleven: Employer Assistance

You may exclude certain educational assistance benefits from your income. That means that you won't have to pay any tax on them. However, it also means that you can't use any of the tax-free education expenses as the basis for any other deduction or credit, including the Hope credit and the lifetime learning credit.

If you receive educational assistance benefits from your employer under an educational assistance program, you can exclude up to $5,250 of those benefits each year. This means your employer should not include the benefits with your wages, tips, and other compensation shown in box 1 of your Form W-2.

To qualify as an educational assistance program, the plan must be written and must meet certain other requirements. Your employer can tell you whether there is a qualified program where you work.

Tax-free educational assistance benefits include payments for tuition, fees and similar expenses, books, supplies, and equipment. The payments may be for either undergraduate- or graduate-level courses. The payments do not have to be for work-related courses. Educational assistance benefits do not include payments for the following items.

- Meals, lodging, or transportation.
- Tools or supplies (other than textbooks) that you can keep after completing the course of instruction.
- Courses involving sports, games, or hobbies unless they:
  - Have a reasonable relationship to the business of your employer, or
  - Are required as part of a degree program.

If your employer pays more than $5,250 for educational benefits for you during the year, you must generally pay tax on the amount over $5,250. Your employer should include in your wages (Form W-2, box 1) the amount that you must include in income.

However, if the benefits over $5,250 also qualify as a working condition fringe benefit, your employer does not have to include them in your wages. A working condition fringe benefit is a benefit which, had you paid for it, you could deduct as an employee business expense.

Chapter Twelve: Business Deductions

If you are an employee and can itemize your deductions, you may be able to claim a deduction for the expenses you pay for your work-related education. Your deduction will be the amount by which your qualifying work-related education expenses plus other job and certain miscellaneous expenses is greater than 2% of your adjusted gross income. An itemized deduction may reduce the amount of your income subject to tax.

If you are self-employed, you deduct your expenses for qualifying work-related education directly from your self-employment income. This may reduce the amount of your income subject to both income tax and self-employment tax.

Your work-related education expenses may also qualify you for other tax benefits, such as the tuition and fees deduction and the Hope and lifetime learning credits. You may qualify for these other benefits even if you do not meet the requirements listed above.

To claim a business deduction for work-related education, you must:
- Be working.
- Itemize your deductions on Schedule A (Form 1040 or 1040NR) if you are an employee.
- File Schedule C (Form 1040), Schedule C-EZ (Form 1040), or Schedule F (Form 1040) if you are self-employed.
- Have expenses for education that meet the requirements discussed under *Qualifying Work-Related Education*, below.

You can deduct the costs of qualifying work-related education as business expenses. This is education that meets at least one of the following two tests:

- The education is required by your employer or the law to keep your present salary, status or job. The required education must serve a bona fide business purpose of your employer.
- The education maintains or improves skills needed in your present work.

However, even if the education meets one or both of the above tests, it is not qualifying work-related education if it:

- Is needed to meet the minimum educational requirements of your present trade or business or
- Is part of a program of study that will qualify you for a new trade or business.

You can deduct the costs of qualifying work-related education as a business expense even if the education could lead to a degree.

Education you need to meet the minimum educational requirements for your present trade or business is not qualifying work-related education. Once you have met the minimum educational requirements for your job, your employer or the law may require you to get more education. This additional education is qualifying work-related education if all three of the following requirements are met.

- It is required for you to keep your present salary, status or job.
- The requirement serves a business purpose of your employer.
- The education is not part of a program that will qualify you for a new trade or business.

When you get more education than your employer or the law requires, the additional education can be qualifying work-related education only if it maintains or improves skills required in your present work.

If your education is not required by your employer or the law, it can be qualifying work-related education only if it maintains or improves skills needed in your present work. This could include refresher courses, courses on current developments and academic or vocational courses.

Chapter Thirteen: IRS Tax Forms

There are several tax forms and worksheets necessary to calculate the various tax credits available. Samples of the more common forms are shown on pages 50 – 53. Complete details are available in IRS Publication 970 and the IRS website, www.irs.gov.

Form 1040

Department of the Treasury—Internal Revenue Service (99)

U.S. Individual Income Tax Return 2014

OMB No. 1545-0074 | IRS Use Only—Do not write or staple in this space.

For the year Jan. 1–Dec. 31, 2014, or other tax year beginning _____, 2014, ending _____, 20 ___ | See separate instructions.

Your first name and initial	Last name		Your social security number

If a joint return, spouse's first name and initial	Last name		Spouse's social security number

Home address (number and street). If you have a P.O. box, see instructions. | Apt. no.

City, town or post office, state, and ZIP code. If you have a foreign address, also complete spaces below (see instructions).

▲ Make sure the SSN(s) above and on line 6c are correct.

Foreign country name	Foreign province/state/county	Foreign postal code

Presidential Election Campaign
Check here if you, or your spouse if filing jointly, want $3 to go to this fund. Checking a box below will not change your tax or refund. ☐ You ☐ Spouse

Filing Status

Check only one box.

1. ☐ Single
2. ☐ Married filing jointly (even if only one had income)
3. ☐ Married filing separately. Enter spouse's SSN above and full name here. ▶
4. ☐ Head of household (with qualifying person). (See instructions.) If the qualifying person is a child but not your dependent, enter this child's name here. ▶
5. ☐ Qualifying widow(er) with dependent child

Exemptions

6a ☐ **Yourself.** If someone can claim you as a dependent, do not check box 6a.
b ☐ **Spouse**

Boxes checked on 6a and 6b ___
No. of children on 6c who:
• lived with you ___
• did not live with you due to divorce or separation (see instructions) ___
Dependents on 6c not entered above ___
Add numbers on lines above ▶ ___

c **Dependents:**

(1) First name Last name	(2) Dependent's social security number	(3) Dependent's relationship to you	(4) ✓ If child under age 17 qualifying for child tax credit (see instructions)
			☐
			☐
			☐
			☐

If more than four dependents, see instructions and check here ▶ ☐

d Total number of exemptions claimed

Income

Attach Form(s) W-2 here. Also attach Forms W-2G and 1099-R if tax was withheld.

If you did not get a W-2, see instructions.

7	Wages, salaries, tips, etc. Attach Form(s) W-2	7	
8a	Taxable interest. Attach Schedule B if required	8a	
b	Tax-exempt interest. Do not include on line 8a	8b	
9a	Ordinary dividends. Attach Schedule B if required	9a	
b	Qualified dividends	9b	
10	Taxable refunds, credits, or offsets of state and local income taxes	10	
11	Alimony received	11	
12	Business income or (loss). Attach Schedule C or C-EZ	12	
13	Capital gain or (loss). Attach Schedule D if required. If not required, check here ▶ ☐	13	
14	Other gains or (losses). Attach Form 4797	14	
15a	IRA distributions	15a		b Taxable amount	15b	
16a	Pensions and annuities	16a		b Taxable amount	16b	
17	Rental real estate, royalties, partnerships, S corporations, trusts, etc. Attach Schedule E	17	
18	Farm income or (loss). Attach Schedule F	18	
19	Unemployment compensation	19	
20a	Social security benefits	20a		b Taxable amount	20b	
21	Other income. List type and amount	21	
22	Combine the amounts in the far right column for lines 7 through 21. This is your **total income** ▶	22	

Adjusted Gross Income

23	Educator expenses	23	
24	Certain business expenses of reservists, performing artists, and fee-basis government officials. Attach Form 2106 or 2106-EZ	24	
25	Health savings account deduction. Attach Form 8889	25	
26	Moving expenses. Attach Form 3903	26	
27	Deductible part of self-employment tax. Attach Schedule SE	27	
28	Self-employed SEP, SIMPLE, and qualified plans	28	
29	Self-employed health insurance deduction	29	
30	Penalty on early withdrawal of savings	30	
31a	Alimony paid b Recipient's SSN ▶	31a	
32	IRA deduction	32	
33	Student loan interest deduction	33	
34	Tuition and fees. Attach Form 8917	34	
35	Domestic production activities deduction. Attach Form 8903	35	
36	Add lines 23 through 35	36	
37	Subtract line 36 from line 22. This is your **adjusted gross income** ▶	37	

For Disclosure, Privacy Act, and Paperwork Reduction Act Notice, see separate instructions. Cat. No. 11320B Form **1040** (2014)

50

Tax and Credits	38	Amount from line 37 (adjusted gross income)	38	
	39a	Check { ☐ You were born before January 2, 1950, ☐ Blind. } Total boxes if { ☐ Spouse was born before January 2, 1950, ☐ Blind. } checked ▶ 39a		
	b	If your spouse itemizes on a separate return or you were a dual-status alien, check here▶ 39b ☐		
Standard Deduction for— • People who check any box on line 39a or 39b or who can be claimed as a dependent, see instructions. • All others: Single or Married filing separately, $6,200 Married filing jointly or Qualifying widow(er), $12,400 Head of household, $9,100	40	**Itemized deductions** (from Schedule A) or your **standard deduction** (see left margin)	40	
	41	Subtract line 40 from line 38	41	
	42	**Exemptions.** If line 38 is $152,525 or less, multiply $3,950 by the number on line 6d. Otherwise, see instructions	42	
	43	**Taxable income.** Subtract line 42 from line 41. If line 42 is more than line 41, enter -0-	43	
	44	Tax (see instructions). Check if any from: a ☐ Form(s) 8814 b ☐ Form 4972 c ☐	44	
	45	**Alternative minimum tax** (see instructions). Attach Form 6251	45	
	46	Excess advance premium tax credit repayment. Attach Form 8962	46	
	47	Add lines 44, 45, and 46 ▶	47	
	48	Foreign tax credit. Attach Form 1116 if required 48		
	49	Credit for child and dependent care expenses. Attach Form 2441 49		
	50	Education credits from Form 8863, line 19 50		
	51	Retirement savings contributions credit. Attach Form 8880 51		
	52	Child tax credit. Attach Schedule 8812, if required 52		
	53	Residential energy credits. Attach Form 5695 53		
	54	Other credits from Form: a ☐ 3800 b ☐ 8801 c ☐ 54		
	55	Add lines 48 through 54. These are your **total credits**	55	
	56	Subtract line 55 from line 47. If line 55 is more than line 47, enter -0- ▶	56	
Other Taxes	57	Self-employment tax. Attach Schedule SE	57	
	58	Unreported social security and Medicare tax from Form: a ☐ 4137 b ☐ 8919	58	
	59	Additional tax on IRAs, other qualified retirement plans, etc. Attach Form 5329 if required	59	
	60a	Household employment taxes from Schedule H	60a	
	b	First-time homebuyer credit repayment. Attach Form 5405 if required	60b	
	61	Health care: individual responsibility (see instructions) Full-year coverage ☐	61	
	62	Taxes from: a ☐ Form 8959 b ☐ Form 8960 c ☐ Instructions; enter code(s)	62	
	63	Add lines 56 through 62. This is your **total tax** ▶	63	
Payments	64	Federal income tax withheld from Forms W-2 and 1099 64		
If you have a qualifying child, attach Schedule EIC.	65	2014 estimated tax payments and amount applied from 2013 return 65		
	66a	Earned income credit (EIC) 66a		
	b	Nontaxable combat pay election 66b		
	67	Additional child tax credit. Attach Schedule 8812 67		
	68	American opportunity credit from Form 8863, line 8 68		
	69	Net premium tax credit. Attach Form 8962 69		
	70	Amount paid with request for extension to file 70		
	71	Excess social security and tier 1 RRTA tax withheld 71		
	72	Credit for federal tax on fuels. Attach Form 4136 72		
	73	Credits from Form: a ☐ 2439 b ☐ Reserved c ☐ Reserved d ☐ 73		
	74	Add lines 64, 65, 66a, and 67 through 73. These are your **total payments** ▶	74	
Refund	75	If line 74 is more than line 63, subtract line 63 from line 74. This is the amount you **overpaid**	75	
	76a	Amount of line 75 you want **refunded to you.** If Form 8888 is attached, check here ▶ ☐	76a	
Direct deposit? See instructions.	▶ b	Routing number	▶ c Type: ☐ Checking ☐ Savings	
	▶ d	Account number		
	77	Amount of line 75 you want applied to your 2015 estimated tax ▶ 77		
Amount You Owe	78	**Amount you owe.** Subtract line 74 from line 63. For details on how to pay, see instructions ▶	78	
	79	Estimated tax penalty (see instructions) 79		
Third Party Designee		Do you want to allow another person to discuss this return with the IRS (see instructions)? ☐ **Yes. Complete below.** ☐ **No** Designee's name ▶ Phone no. ▶ Personal identification number (PIN) ▶		
Sign Here Joint return? See instructions. Keep a copy for your records.		Under penalties of perjury, I declare that I have examined this return and accompanying schedules and statements, and to the best of my knowledge and belief, they are true, correct, and complete. Declaration of preparer (other than taxpayer) is based on all information of which preparer has any knowledge. Your signature Date Your occupation Daytime phone number Spouse's signature. If a joint return, both must sign. Date Spouse's occupation If the IRS sent you an Identity Protection PIN, enter it here (see inst.)		
Paid Preparer Use Only		Print/Type preparer's name Preparer's signature Date Check ☐ if self-employed PTIN Firm's name ▶ Firm's EIN ▶ Firm's address ▶ Phone no.		

Form 8863

Department of the Treasury
Internal Revenue Service (99)

Education Credits
(American Opportunity and Lifetime Learning Credits)
▶ Attach to Form 1040 or Form 1040A.
▶ Information about Form 8863 and its separate instructions is at www.irs.gov/form8863.

OMB No. 1545-0074

2014

Attachment
Sequence No. **50**

Name(s) shown on return

Your social security number

⚠ **CAUTION** Complete a separate Part III on page 2 for each student for whom you are claiming either credit before you complete Parts I and II.

Part I Refundable American Opportunity Credit

1	After completing Part III for each student, enter the total of all amounts from all Parts III, line 30	**1**	
2	Enter: $180,000 if married filing jointly; $90,000 if single, head of household, or qualifying widow(er)	**2**	
3	Enter the amount from Form 1040, line 38, or Form 1040A, line 22. If you are filing Form 2555, 2555-EZ, or 4563, or you are excluding income from Puerto Rico, see Pub. 970 for the amount to enter	**3**	
4	Subtract line 3 from line 2. If zero or less, **stop**; you cannot take any education credit	**4**	
5	Enter: $20,000 if married filing jointly; $10,000 if single, head of household, or qualifying widow(er)	**5**	
6	If line 4 is: • Equal to or more than line 5, enter 1.000 on line 6 • Less than line 5, divide line 4 by line 5. Enter the result as a decimal (rounded to at least three places)	**6**	.
7	Multiply line 1 by line 6. **Caution:** If you were under age 24 at the end of the year and meet the conditions described in the instructions, you **cannot** take the refundable American opportunity credit; skip line 8, enter the amount from line 7 on line 9, and check this box ▶ ☐	**7**	
8	**Refundable American opportunity credit.** Multiply line 7 by 40% (.40). Enter the amount here and on Form 1040, line 68, or Form 1040A, line 44. Then go to line 9 below.	**8**	

Part II Nonrefundable Education Credits

9	Subtract line 8 from line 7. Enter here and on line 2 of the Credit Limit Worksheet (see instructions)	**9**	
10	After completing Part III for each student, enter the total of all amounts from all Parts III, line 31. If zero, skip lines 11 through 17, enter -0- on line 18, and go to line 19	**10**	
11	Enter the smaller of line 10 or $10,000	**11**	
12	Multiply line 11 by 20% (.20)	**12**	
13	Enter: $128,000 if married filing jointly; $64,000 if single, head of household, or qualifying widow(er)	**13**	
14	Enter the amount from Form 1040, line 38, or Form 1040A, line 22. If you are filing Form 2555, 2555-EZ, or 4563, or you are excluding income from Puerto Rico, see Pub. 970 for the amount to enter	**14**	
15	Subtract line 14 from line 13. If zero or less, skip lines 16 and 17, enter -0- on line 18, and go to line 19 ▶	**15**	
16	Enter: $20,000 if married filing jointly; $10,000 if single, head of household, or qualifying widow(er)	**16**	
17	If line 15 is: • Equal to or more than line 16, enter 1.000 on line 17 and go to line 18 • Less than line 16, divide line 15 by line 16. Enter the result as a decimal (rounded to at least three places)	**17**	.
18	Multiply line 12 by line 17. Enter here and on line 1 of the Credit Limit Worksheet (see instructions) ▶	**18**	
19	**Nonrefundable education credits.** Enter the amount from line 7 of the Credit Limit Worksheet (see instructions) here and on Form 1040, line 50, or Form 1040A, line 33	**19**	

For Paperwork Reduction Act Notice, see your tax return instructions.   Cat. No. 25379M   Form **8863** (2014)

52

Form **8815**	**Exclusion of Interest From Series EE and I U.S. Savings Bonds Issued After 1989** (For Filers With Qualified Higher Education Expenses) ▶ Information about Form 8815 and its instructions is at www.irs.gov/form8815. ▶ Attach to Form 1040 or Form 1040A.	OMB No. 1545-0074 **2014**
Department of the Treasury Internal Revenue Service (99)		Attachment Sequence No. **167**

Name(s) shown on return / Your social security number

1 (a) Name of person (you, your spouse, or your dependent) who was enrolled at or attended an eligible educational institution	(b) Name and address of eligible educational institution

If you need more space, attach a statement.

2	Enter the total qualified higher education expenses you paid in 2014 for the person(s) listed in column (a) of line 1. See the instructions to find out which expenses qualify	2	
3	Enter the total of any nontaxable educational benefits (such as nontaxable scholarship or fellowship grants) received for 2014 for the person(s) listed in column (a) of line 1 (see instructions)	3	
4	Subtract line 3 from line 2. If zero or less, **stop.** You **cannot** take the exclusion	4	
5	Enter the total proceeds (principal and interest) from all series EE and I U.S. savings bonds **issued after 1989** that you **cashed during 2014**	5	
6	Enter the interest included on line 5 (see instructions)	6	
7	If line 4 is equal to or more than line 5, enter "1.000." If line 4 is less than line 5, divide line 4 by line 5. Enter the result as a decimal (rounded to at least three places)	7	× .
8	Multiply line 6 by line 7	8	
9	Enter your modified adjusted gross income (see instructions)	9	
	Note: If line 9 is $91,000 or more if single or head of household, or $143,950 or more if married filing jointly or qualifying widow(er) with dependent child, **stop.** You **cannot** take the exclusion.		
10	Enter: $76,000 if single or head of household; $113,950 if married filing jointly or qualifying widow(er) with dependent child	10	
11	Subtract line 10 from line 9. If zero or less, skip line 12, enter -0- on line 13, and go to line 14	11	
12	Divide line 11 by: $15,000 if single or head of household; $30,000 if married filing jointly or qualifying widow(er) with dependent child. Enter the result as a decimal (rounded to at least three places)	12	× .
13	Multiply line 8 by line 12	13	
14	**Excludable savings bond interest.** Subtract line 13 from line 8. Enter the result here and on Schedule B (Form 1040A or 1040), line 3 . . . . ▶	14	

For Paperwork Reduction Act Notice, see your tax return instructions.　　Cat. No. 10822S　　Form **8815** (2014)

Chapter Fourteen: Questions & Answers

Q1. Are there any changes to the tax credits for college expenses?

A. The American opportunity tax credit, which expanded and renamed the already-existing Hope credit, can be claimed for tuition and certain fees you pay for higher education in 2009 and 2010.

Q2. The Hope credit originally applied only to the first two years of college. Has that changed?

A. Yes. The American opportunity tax credit can be claimed for expenses for the first four years of post-secondary education.

Q3. How much is the American opportunity tax credit worth?

A. It is a tax credit of up to $2,500 of the cost of qualified tuition and related expenses paid during the taxable year. That is a $700 increase from the previous Hope credit.

Q4. What education expenses qualify for the American opportunity tax credit?

A. The term "qualified tuition and related expenses" has been expanded to include expenditures for "course materials." For this purpose, the term "course materials" means books, supplies and equipment needed for a course of study whether or not the materials are purchased from the educational institution as a condition of enrollment or attendance.

Q5. Does an expenditure for a computer qualify for the American opprtunity tax credit?

A. Whether an expenditure for a computer qualifies for the credit depends on the facts. An expenditure for a computer would qualify for the credit if the computer is needed for enrollment or attendance at the educational institution.

Q6. How is the American opportunity tax credit calculated?

A. Taxpayers will receive a tax credit based on 100 percent of the first $2,000 of tuition, fees and course materials paid during the taxable year, plus 25 percent of the next $2,000 of tuition, fees and course materials paid during the taxable year.

Q7. How will the American opportunity tax credit affect my income tax return?

A. You will be able to reduce your tax liability one dollar for each dollar of credit for which you're eligible. If the amount of the American opportunity tax credit for which you're eligible is more than your tax liability, the amount of the credit that is more than your tax liability is refundable to you, up to a maximum refund of 40 percent of the amount of the credit for which you're eligible.

Q8. Who is eligible for the American opportunity tax credit?

A. A taxpayer who pays qualified tuition and related expenses and whose federal income tax return has a modified adjusted gross income of $80,000 or less ($160,000 or less for joint filers) is eligible for the credit. The credit is reduced ratably if a taxpayer's modified adjusted gross income exceeds those amounts. A taxpayer whose modified adjusted gross income is greater than $90,000 ($180,000 for joint filers) cannot benefit from this credit.

Q9. What is "modified adjusted gross income" for the purposes of the American opportunity tax credit?

A. It is the taxpayer's adjusted gross income increased by foreign income that was excluded, and by income excluded from sources in Puerto Rico or certain U.S. possessions.

Q10. How is the credit claimed?

A. The credit is claimed using Form 8863, attached to Form 1040 or 1040A.

Q11. I'm just beginning college this year. Can I claim the American opportunity tax credit for all four years I pay tuition?

A. The American opportunity tax credit is for amounts paid in 2009 and 2010 only. You may be eligible for the lifetime learning credit for any tuition and fees required for enrollment you pay after 2010.

Q12. Can I also claim the tuition and fees tax deduction in addition to claiming the American opportunity tax credit?

A. No. You cannot claim the tuition and fees tax deduction in the same year that you claim the American opportunity tax credit or the lifetime learning credit. You must choose among them. You also cannot claim the tuition and fees tax deduction if anyone else claims the American opportunity tax credit or the lifetime learning credit for you in the same year. A tax deduction of up to $4,000 can be claimed for qualified tuition and fees paid. Though the credit will usually result in greater tax savings, taxpayers should calculate the effect of both on the tax return to see which is most beneficial — the tax credit or the deduction. Often tax software will automatically compare the two for you.

American Opportunity Credit: Questions and Answers

October 10, 2009

http://www.irs.gov/newsroom/article/0,,id=211309,00.html